Revolutionary W

Author   Linda Milliken
Illustrator   Barb Lorseyedi

EP107 © GHC Specialty Brands, LLC, 1996, 2007
401 S. Wright Road
Janesville, WI 53547

Table of Contents

The Hands-on Heritage series has been designed to help you bring culture to life in your classroom! Look for the "For the Teacher" headings to find information to help you prepare for activities. Simply block out these sections when reproducing pages for student use.

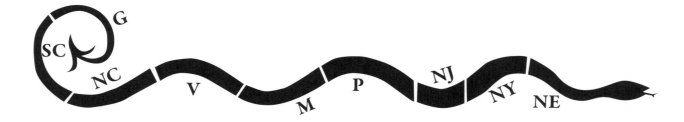

Introduction

The Revolutionary War was not the result of a single, particular event, but rather the culmination of a series of escalating incidences. It began with a proclamation issued by King George of England—American colonists were not to establish settlements west of the Appalachian Mountains.

The British then proceeded to pass a number of laws that angered the colonists. Included was a law that forbade the colonists from printing their own currency. Then a series of burdensome tax laws were imposed, which angered the colonists even more. The Americans felt the British were being unfair, while the British view was that the taxation benefitted the businesses of England.

Rebellious Patriots directed other events that lead to the war, including the Boston Massacre, the Boston Tea Party, and the meeting of the First Continental Congress. Finally, the first shot was fired at Lexington, where a group of armed colonists tried to resist British soldiers from seizing an American arsenal. This shot at Lexington is known as "the shot heard 'round the world."

For the Teacher

Project
Create a time line of incidents and/or events that precipitated the Revolutionary War.

Materials
- research materials
- lined index cards
- pen/pencil
- butcher paper (any color)
- push pins
- white drawing paper or construction paper
- crayons or colored pencils
- black marker

Directions
1. Divide class into small groups.
2. Use the information in the box to assign each group an event or incident to research.
3. Cover a bulletin board with butcher paper.
4. Draw a black line across the middle of the butcher paper to create the time line.
5. Have students write a short explanation of the event or a description of the incident on a lined index card.
6. Attach index cards, with the date, in correct order on the time line.
7. Have students make a simple drawing or representation of the information on the index card. Attach above the card.

Time Line
1763—Proclamation of 1763 Issued
1764—British Impose New Taxes
1765—Stamp Act Passed
1767—Townshend Acts Passed
1767—Colonists Respond with Boycott
1768—British Troops Land in Boston
1770—Boston Massacre
1773—Boston Tea Party
1774—Intolerable Acts Imposed
1774—First Continental Congress Meets
1775—"Shot Heard 'Round the World"

Farming

During the Revolutionary War era, owning land was the goal of most Americans. Farmers who made their living from the land wished to pass the ownership on to their children. Those who owned land were called *freeholders* or *yeomen*.

Farmers' tools were simple, and their use required heavy labor. Fields were tilled with wooden plows pulled by oxen. Seeds were sown by hand. At harvest time, crops were cut with a hand-held sickle. On the family farm, women and children were valuable workers.

Project

Sow seeds by hand like a Revolutionary War-era farmer. Watch your garden grow.

Materials

- seedling trays or egg cartons
- premixed potting soil and fertilizer
- variety of seeds
- small gardening tools or spoons
- newspapers
- scissors
- index card
- black fine-tipped marker
- water
- foam cups

Directions

1. Cover work area with newspaper.
2. If using egg cartons, cut off the tops.
3. Place soil in egg carton sections or several seedling-tray sections.
4. Plant seeds one by one and water.
5. Write your name and identify the seeds you planted on an index card.
6. Tend your garden and watch it grow!
7. Repot in larger containers if necessary.

   EP107 Revolutionary War Era © GHC Specialty Brands, LLC

Craftsmen

Nearly 100,000 Americans were living in major cities along the Atlantic coast in 1774–1775. Half these people were craftsmen aspiring to become masters of trades, such as silversmiths, furniture builders, shipbuilders, blacksmiths, printers, tailors, and engravers. A skilled craftsman often incorporated the symbols of the new nation into his creations. Eagles were often carved on furniture as well as on ships' bows. It was common to put a personal marking on a product as well.

Men skilled in their craft were known as mechanics, tradesmen, or "leather aprons." The last name came from the heavy leather aprons many craftsmen wore as protection from injuries that could result from their work.

Project

Make a "leather apron" from butcher paper.

Materials

- brown butcher paper
- black or brown tempera paint
- paintbrush
- scissors
- measuring tape
- stapler
- thick yarn

Directions

1. Work with a partner to measure the distance from waistline to just above the knees.

2. Cut a piece of butcher paper into a rectangle the length of the measurement and approximately 18 inches (46 cm) wide.

3. Paint the butcher paper rectangle to create a "worn" look. Crumple the edges and cut a slit in the front.

4. Fold the top 2 inches (5 cm) of the butcher paper over yarn cut long enough to fit around the waist and tie in a bow. Staple the yarn and butcher paper together to hold in place.

Masters and Apprentices

The practice of indenturing boys was common during Revolutionary times. An indentured boy was pledged to learn a craft and remain unmarried. He signed a contract stating this intent and became an *apprentice*, obligated to his *master*, a craftsman skilled in his trade with his own business. In exchange for work, the master provided food and lodging and the promise that his skills would be shared with and taught to his apprentice.

When an apprentice completed his contract, he became a *journeyman* and was eligible to earn wages. If he was able to save enough money, he could become a master.

Project

Work in pairs, as master and apprentice, and complete a Revolutionary-era craft.

Materials

- Revolutionary Crafts Project Page
- various materials as specified on each card
- books about Revolutionary-era crafts

Directions

1. Select a Revolutionary Craft Card and gather all the materials necessary to complete the project.
2. Share completed projects and a few facts about your "profession."

For the Teacher

1. Reproduce several sets of the Revolutionary Craft Cards (page 7) and cut them apart. Review the cards and discuss each project.
2. Divide into cooperative pairs, a "master" and an "apprentice."

Revolutionary Crafts Project Page

Silversmith

Most towns had a silversmith who made valuable pieces of silverware such as candlesticks, medals, and coffee or tea pots.

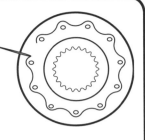

- Use cardboard and aluminum foil to create a platter, tray, bowl, or cup.
- Use a toothpick to engrave designs in the foil. Engrave the initials of the silversmith as well.

Engraver

Before cameras were invented, important events were recreated through the technique of engraving.

- Create an "engraving." Brush a thick layer of black tempera paint on white paper.
- Use a toothpick to draw a picture in the paint. Create a paper frame for the engraving.

Printer

The printer selected metal type, inked it, then pressed it onto paper to create words and sentences, letter by letter.

- Fold a large sheet of construction paper into four sections.
- Cut out individual letters from magazines and paste them to the construction paper to create a newspaper.

Carpenter

Master woodworkers constructed buildings and made tables, chairs, and other furnishings.

- Use building materials to construct a shelf, box, or other woodworking project.
- Learn how to sand and finish. (You might even try stenciling a design on the fini[sh] project!)

Clockmakers

Clockmakers carved gears from brass and pewter disks. They sold only clockworks and faces. A cabinetmaker made the case.

- Combine the skills of a clockmaker and cabinetmaker to make a clock. Use paper and a cereal box to cut, glue, and create a clock face with a fancy case.

Shipbuilder

Wooden ships were built in every seaport on the Atlantic coast. Shipwri[ghts] bolted timbers toge[ther] and bent planks t[o] frames.

- Use lumb[er,] sticks, t[...] tools[...]
- Tes[t ...]

Women

The life of women during the Revolutionary War era revolved around the home. Girls married at a young age, and as wives and mothers they had many responsibilities. Women spent their days preparing food, tending livestock, supervising farm work, and making the household clothes and linens. Few women had careers outside their homes. However, some women taught children in schools, tended shops or taverns, or worked as seamstresses.

Dairying, or tending to the family cows and their milk products, was a full-time job. One chore that was often shared by women and children was butter-making. Cream was poured into a wooden or earthenware keg, called a *churn*. The keg was fitted with a tight lid in which there was a hole. The handle of a paddle, or *dasher*, was fit through the hole. As the dasher was pushed up and down, butterfat was removed from the milk, eventually forming a lump of butter.

There are also stories of women who took part in the Revolutionary War. Margaret Corbin went to war with her husband. When he was killed in battle she took over the firing of his cannon. Molly Hays became known as Molly Pitcher when she carried water to the soldiers on the battlefield. Deborah Sampson disguised herself as a man and fought as a soldier.

For the Teacher

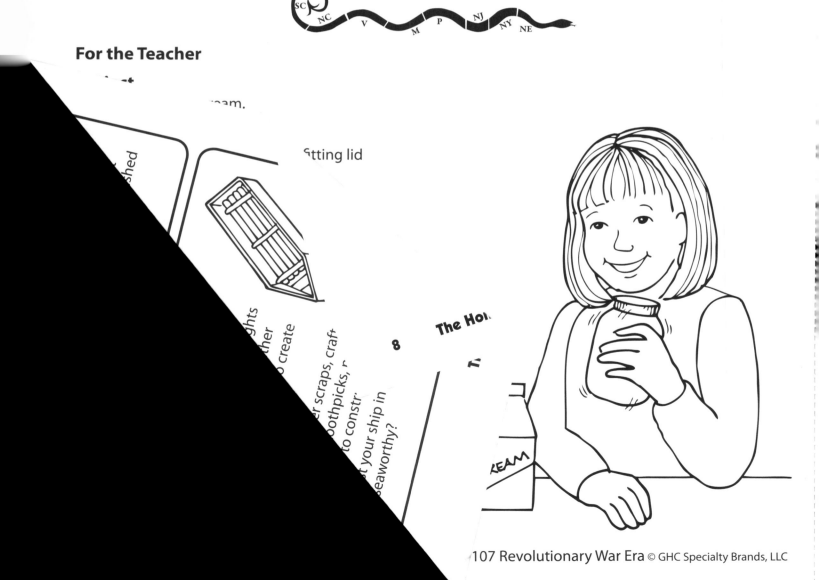

Women's "Pockets"

A woman during the Revolutionary era carried her belongings around in a *pocket*, a cloth bag tied around her waist, usually under her skirt. Pockets could be very plain or very ornate. Some were made of patchwork or were decorated with beautiful embroidery. A pocket might contain keys, sewing thread, pins, needles, or a baby's bib.

Project

Design a pocket and fill it with objects used by a Revolutionary War-era woman.

Materials

- two pieces fabric, 8 x 12 inches (20 x 30 cm)
- needle, thread
- ribbon or yarn
- scissors
- household items

Directions

1. Cut two pocket shapes from fabric. Cut a slit down the middle of one pocket, cutting about one-third of the way from the top.
2. With needle and thread, join pocket pieces.
3. Fold over top of pocket 1 inch (2.54 cm) and sew to form a casing.
4. Measure yarn or ribbon to go around waist, with excess to tie a bow. Thread through casing.
5. Fill pocket with household items that may have been used by a woman in Revolutionary War times.

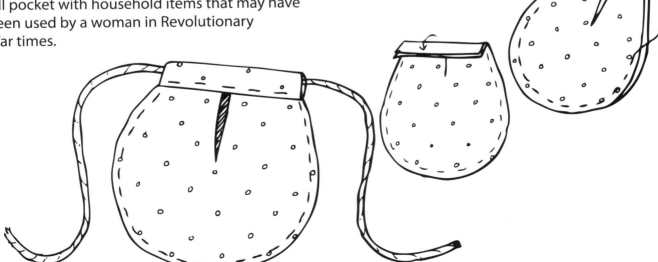

Food and Cooking

The kitchen fireplace was used for all cooking tasks. An iron pot hung from a crane. Frying was done in a long-handled iron skillet, called a *spider*, that stood high on three legs. Roasting was done on a spit inside a sheet-iron box with one open side facing the fire. Baking was done in a fireplace built in the wall, next to the main fireplace. A stove was used strictly for heating.

People ate large quantities of animal fat, and few green vegetables and fruits. Diseases such as scurvy, rickets, and cholera were common. Food spoiled quickly without means for storing it properly. Frozen ice from ponds provided minimal cooling.

Project

Prepare simple foods to serve at a Revolutionary War-era meal.

Materials

- see ingredients for individual recipes
- mixing bowls, spatulas, measuring cups, and spoons
- paper plates
- plastic forks and knives
- white butcher paper

Directions

1. Review the recipes. Divide into cooperative groups to plan and carry out the tasks of food and table preparation.

2. Serve the meal as if you were in a wealthy Revolutionary-era home. Set the table with a white butcher paper "cloth" and a plate for everyone. Lay a fork on the table, tines down, to the left of the plate. Set a knife to the right of the plate. (No napkins were used; mouths were wiped with the edge of the tablecloth!)

For the Teacher

Assign individual tasks or have students work in groups. Assist students in preparing recipes. Copy enough Recipe Projects (page 11) for each student or group.

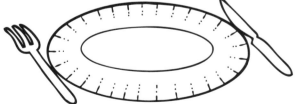

Recipe Project Page

Cider

Most men started the day with a "draft" of hard cider, beer, or whiskey and water. Other beverages were tea and coffee.

Directions

1. Heat **water** in a pan on a hot plate. Place several **tea bags** in the hot water to brew tea. Ladle the hot tea into foam or heat-sensitive cups.
2. Offer an alternate drink: cold **apple cider.**

Cornbread

Bread was served at most meals. Butter was often sliced and eaten like cheese. The poor put molasses on bread instead of butter.

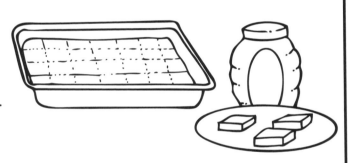

Directions

1. Make **cornbread** according to package directions.
2. Serve with **butter** slices and small cups of **molasses** for experimental "dipping."

Blood Pudding

Less fortunate people had especially poor diets. Their meat, called blood pudding, consisted of beef and pig blood cooked with meat scraps and stuffed into sausage skins. With it they ate bread and molasses. A prosperous family would dine on eight or 10 food items, including boiled goose and roasted turkey.

Directions

1. Cut **sausage** into slices.
2. Lightly fry in an electric skillet.
3. Spoon into a large bowl for serving.

Dining

A formal dinner in a wealthy home lasted three or four hours. Plates were porcelain, spoons were silver, elegant rounded knives and three-tined forks were steel with silver or bone handles. A dinner plate stayed on a warming rack until needed. When forks were introduced, napkins were eliminated; guests wiped their mouths with the tablecloth. Sometimes finger bowls were used. Many well-mannered people used the blade of the knife for transferring food from plate to mouth.

Simpler homes owned blue-printed pottery, or cream-colored Wedgewood™. Plates with "American scenes" on them also were popular.

Project
Paint a dinner plate with an American scene.

Materials
- paper plates
- pencils
- watercolor paints and brushes

Directions
1. Brainstorm a list of images that remind you of a typical "American scene." For example: children in a classroom; parents at a soccer field.
2. Choose a scene from the list and sketch it on a paper plate.
3. Use watercolor paints to complete the sketch. Add an edge of bright green or blue paint.

For the Teacher
Display the plates on a bulletin board.

Education

There was no free public education during the Revolutionary era. Parents who wanted their children educated had to pay for it. Many wanted their children to read so they could study the Bible, often the only book a family owned. Ordinary people and poor families did not have the money to pay for a teacher. More importantly, children were needed to help with the work. Country families would often hire one tutor for the entire community.

City boys decided on a trade and became apprentices to become master craftsmen. Wealthy families sent their sons to college. Girls learned the skills required for parenting and home management.

Project
Make a book cover similar to those used by Revolutionary-era school children.

Materials
- brown paper bag
- clear tape or masking tape
- double-stick Velcro®
- scissors
- ruler
- pencil

Directions
1. Cut the paper bag open and lay it flat.
2. Choose a book to cover. Open the book and lay it on top of the paper bag. Mark the bag with a line along the top and bottom edges of the book. Measure 4 inches (10 cm) from the edges of the book. Cut along the lines to create a rectangle.
3. Fold one end in at the 4-inch (10 cm) mark and tape the top and bottom closed. Cut the other end to create a tab, as shown.

4. Slide the book jacket into the folded end. Wrap the tab end over the closed book. Place a small piece of double-stick Velcro® on the tab and book cover where they meet.

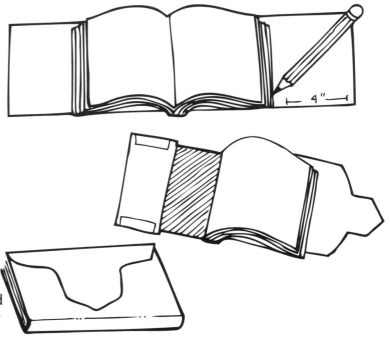

Extension Activity
Noah Webster wrote the first American speller in 1783. The cost? Fourteen cents. The speller was popular for more than 100 years and sold more than 100 million copies. Webster also wrote a grammar book and a dictionary. Look in your home and classroom libraries to see if you have a modern version of Webster's dictionary.

Clothing

Clothing of the Revolutionary era was generally made of linen, wool, or a combination of these, called linsey-woolsey.

Men of the Revolutionary era wore skirted coats, and tricorn (three-cornered) hats. With these, they wore long stockings and leather shoes decorated with metal buckles. They sometimes wore white-powdered wigs, although by 1776, many men preferred to powder their own hair white instead. Work clothes and clothing worn by farmers included loose-fitting smocks and loose breeches.

Women wore dresses with long, bell-shaped skirts. The sleeves were generally elbow-length, and sometimes trimmed with linen ruffles. Over their shoulders they often wore a triangular piece of fabric called a kerchief. They also often wore buckled shoes and caps. For very formal wear, women might also wear powdered wigs or powder their hair. Clothing for wear in the city or for church was a bit more stylish.

Children dressed in the same styles as adults, with the exception of very young children, who wore long smocks or aprons.

Project

Recreate the clothing styles of Revolutionary-era men and women.

Directions

Choose a project from the Clothing Project Page and follow directions. Model clothing.

For the Teacher

Copy one Women's Clothing Project Page (15) or Men's Clothing Page (16) for each student.

Women's Clothing Project Page

Women

1. Borrow long, full skirts and aprons from parents.
2. Fold a 36-inch (1-m) square of fabric in half diagonally. Wrap around shoulders, securing with a safety pin in front.
3. Cover two 2-inch (5-cm) squares of cardboard with aluminum foil and attach to shoes.
4. Follow directions to make cap.

Cap

Directions

1. Cut a circle from a 24-inch (61-cm) square of fabric.
2. Sew a casing of seam binding 2 inches (5-cm) from the edge of circle.
3. Measure elastic to fit student's head plus 1 inch (2.54 cm).
4. Run elastic through casing and secure.

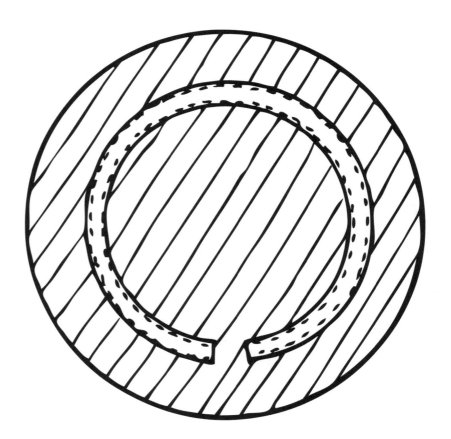

Men's Clothing Project Page

Men

1. Roll up long pant legs to just below the knee and secure with a rubber band.
2. Wear long sports socks and secure under edges of pant legs.
3. Cover two 2-inch (5-cm) squares of cardboard with aluminum foil and attach to shoes.
4. Follow directions to make a three-cornered hat.

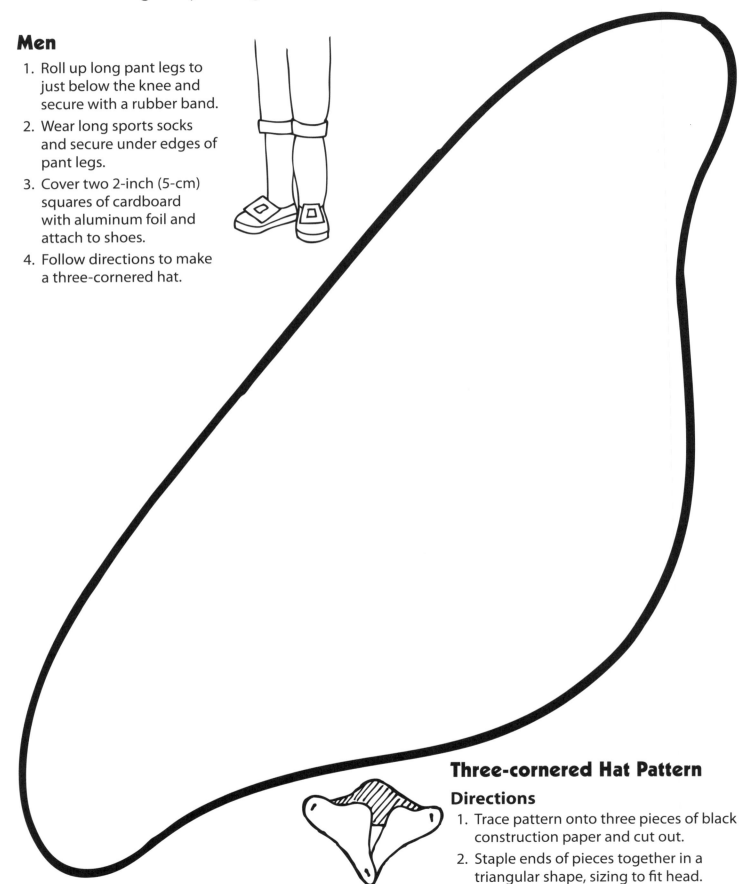

Three-cornered Hat Pattern

Directions

1. Trace pattern onto three pieces of black construction paper and cut out.
2. Staple ends of pieces together in a triangular shape, sizing to fit head.

Postal Service

The Second Continental Congress officially established a postal system in 1775. Mail was packed in coarse bags made from a heavy woven material. The bags were carried by stagecoaches that had established regular lines from city to city, advertising their routes in the newspapers. Mail for small villages with no post office was left at a store or an inn. No stamps existed. An addressee usually paid the postage when he received the letter. Distance, not weight, determined the postage. There were no envelopes or postcards. The letter was folded twice and twice again and held with a blob of sealing wax. Sometimes an engraved seal was stamped into the wax.

For the Teacher

Project

Establish a Revolutionary-era postal system in the classroom.

Materials

- burlap
- large needle
- thick yarn
- plain writing paper
- stickers
- poker chips or other "coins"

Directions

1. Make one large mail bag for classroom use. Cut the burlap into a large rectangle, 24 x 60 inches (61 cm x 1.5 m). Fold it in half and stitch the sides with yarn. Fold over the top and stitch to create a casing. Thread yarn through the casing to make a shoulder strap.

2. Hang the mail bag in the classroom. Choose a different post carrier for each day.

3. Students write letters, folding them as shown in the illustration and sealing them with a sticker. They can then deposit the letters in the mail bag for delivery.

4. The post carrier must collect one chip when the letter is delivered. The chips should be deposited in one location to be reused.

Children

At the time of the Revolutionary War, almost one-half of all Americans were younger than 16 years of age. There were many large families in spite of the fact that quite a few children never survived childhood because of disease, poor diets, and inadequate medical care. It wasn't unusual for families to have 10 to 12 children, especially those who owned farms. Most children who went to school, walking as far as three miles each way, learned to read, write, and "do sums."

It was a new American idea for a man to divide his estate among all his children, rather than passing it on to his eldest son. Marriage for girls, as early as 15 years of age, was the general rule.

Project
Create an item that a Revolutionary child might have owned.

For the Teacher
Copy one set of Children's Project Pages (18–19) per student.

Materials
- Children Project Pages
- see individual projects

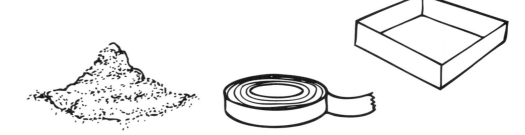

Slates

Children practiced writing and sums on small slates. If a slate was not available, the children spread sand on boards and wrote in it with their fingertips.

Materials
- gift box lid
- sand or loose dirt
- masking tape

Directions
1. Tape the corners of the box lid to strengthen them.
2. Pour about ¼ inch (.6 cm) of sand in the lid.
3. Use your "sand-slate" for your responses during a class spelling or math lesson.

EP107 Revolutionary War Era © GHC Specialty Brands, LLC

Children Project Page

Porringer

A porringer, a small bowl usually crafted from pewter, was often given as a gift to a child at birth. Well-to-do families presented porringers crafted from silver. American-made porringers featured a carved handle similar to the shape of a crown.

Materials

- paper bowl
- aluminium foil
- lightweight cardboard
- scissors
- tape

Directions

1. Cut a handle shape, as shown, from the cardboard. Cut a slot in the bowl and insert the handle into the slot. Use tape to hold the handle in place.
2. Cover the bowl and handle with aluminum foil.

Wooden Doll

Children played with toys made from simple materials. While some dolls were made from leather, most were created with wood. A "penny wooden" doll was distinguished by its wooden joints and a peg on top of its head.

Materials

- old-fashioned wooden clothespin
- fabric scraps
- thin-tipped markers
- scissors
- rubber bands
- yarn
- needle, thread
- glue

Directions

1. Use markers to draw a face on the clothespin head.
2. Fashion clothing from the fabric scraps. Sew with needle and thread, or glue fabric pieces together.
3. Dress the doll in the clothes. A rubber band may hold the clothing in place.
4. Add yarn hair.

Sampler

Needlework was important to Revolutionary-era women in cities and on farms. As soon as a young girl was able to hold a needle, she began practicing her sewing skills. One way she did this was with a *sampler*, a small square or strip of cloth covered with different needlework patterns.

Letters, numerals, quotations, and verses were stitched into the sampler. Sometimes a girl would add her name, age, and the date the sampler was made. Samplers eventually became part of a girl's formal instruction and became evidence of educational accomplishments. Many styles and shapes of samplers were produced in the United States until the end of the 1800s.

Project
Create a mock cross-stitch sampler on graph paper.

Materials
- graph paper
- lightweight white paper
- colored pencils
- half-sheet colored construction paper
- glue

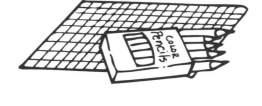

Directions
1. Reproduce the graph paper on lightweight white paper.
2. Simulate a cross-stitch by making an "X" in each square with a colored pencil. Place the "stitches" on the graph paper to spell out the alphabet, your name, or a design.
3. Display the sampler by mounting it on a colored construction paper frame.

For the Teacher
Copy one Sampler Graph Paper (page 21) per student.

Sampler Graph Paper

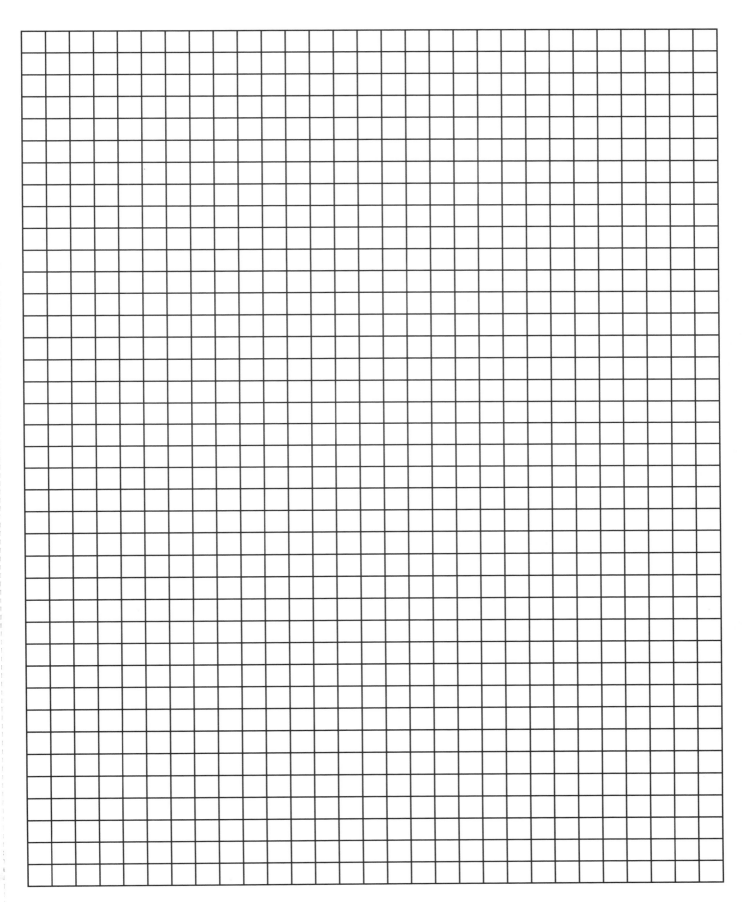

Handbills

The primary way that political opinions and news about events could be spread was through the printed word. Thirty-seven newspapers were being published in the colonies in 1775. Most were four-page, tabloid-size papers that were published weekly. The average circulation was 500 copies. By 1790, there were more than 90 newspapers in the country, and by 1810, there were about 375.

A *handbill*, or *broadside*, was a single page that a printer could quickly reproduce to be posted on trees or tavern doors. Its purpose was to report the latest news from Europe or to encourage people to come to a meeting. A handbill was often done in cartoon style, expressing dissatisfaction with government policies.

Project
Create a handbill to post at school.

Materials
- sheet of plain writing paper
- black markers
- photocopy machine
- masking tape

Directions
1. Create a black and white, one-page handbill that announces an important school or community event.
2. Add pictures and create text to draw attention to the handbill.

For the Teacher
Tape the handbills around school for students to share and read. Don't forget to take them down after a few days!

> **Extension Activity**
> Look through newspapers for editorial cartoons. Create a "Current Events" board featuring the newspaper clippings.

Flatboat

In the late 1700s, transporting people and cargo by river on flat-bottomed barges, called *flatboats*, proved to be the cheapest and easiest way to travel.

Flatboats were built from long planks. They measured up to 50 feet (15.2 m) long and about 15 feet (4.6 m) wide. Their narrow width enabled them to travel the channels of the Ohio and Mississippi rivers. One end of the flatboat had a sheltered area for sleeping and eating. Some had fences around the sides for protection. Because they drifted with the current, guided by long poles, flatboats could only travel one way. They were taken apart at the end of the trip and the lumber was used for other purposes, often to build homes for the passengers.

Project

Construct a replica of a flatboat.

Materials

- small gift box, approximately 3 inches (7.6 cm) square
- shoebox lid
- brown tempera paint
- paintbrush
- scissors
- glue
- craft sticks
- optional: two long twigs, masking tape

Directions

1. Cut open one side of the gift box.
2. Paint the craft sticks and gift box. Invert the shoe box lid so that the top becomes the bottom of the flatboat. Paint the sides of the lid.
3. When the paint has dried, glue craft sticks to cover the inside of the lid, breaking the sticks to fit.

4. Glue the gift box toward one end of the "flatboat." If you can find two long twigs, tape them to the top of the gift box, as shown in the illustration.

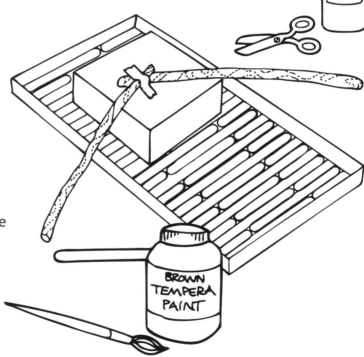

Extension Activity

- Brainstorm a list of uses for the lumber made available when a flatboat was torn apart. What goods and services might Revolutionary travelers have needed in their new homes?
- Conduct experiments involving currents. How can you make an object move against the flow of water?

Tree of Liberty

In 1765, the people of Boston designated a giant elm on the main road into town as their Tree of Liberty, where demonstrations opposing British rule and policies were held. Other colonists followed this example and set aside a Liberty Tree in their towns to serve as a central meeting place where grievances could be expressed.

The image of the Tree of Liberty began appearing all over the colonies, on posters, engravings, and soldiers' equipment. It became the most common colonial symbol of the American Revolution.

Project
Paint a Tree of Liberty.

Materials
- watercolor paints
- crayons
- white construction paper
- paintbrushes

Directions
1. Use the chalkboard drawing as a model for individual watercolor resist paintings.
2. Heavily color a Tree of Liberty on white construction paper.
3. Paint over the drawing with a watercolor wash of red or blue.
4. Write a paragraph defining the meaning of liberty.

For the Teacher
1. Recreate the picture of the Tree of Liberty, as illustrated, on the chalkboard.
2. Feature the paintings in a display next to student-written paragraphs defining the meaning of liberty.

Liberty Pole

Some colonies did not have giant elms in the center of their town to dedicate as "Liberty Trees." These people found it just as patriotic to erect a giant pole in the center of town. These colonists identified their symbol as a "Liberty Pole," exemplifying their patriotism just as much as the original Tree of Liberty in Boston. Frequently, these poles were adorned with the flags of the colonies.

Project

As a class, create a "Liberty Pole" to represent unity, as the American colonists did during the Revolutionary War.

Materials

- research materials
- variety of colored construction paper
- colored markers or crayons
- scissors
- three cardboard tubes from wrapping paper
- duct tape
- yarn
- stapler

Directions

1. In small groups, research places, people, objects, or events that represent your town or city.
2. Create flags with symbols and colors that depicts your town or city.
3. Fasten the cardboard tubes together with duct tape.
4. Tape brown construction paper around the tubes to simulate a wooden pole.
5. Thread a piece of yarn through the open ends of the tube. Tie the ends together to form a loop.
6. Staple all the flags to the yarn.
7. Take turns explaining the significance of your flags.

Choosing a Militia

When General George Washington of Virginia took command of the Continental Army, he requested 500 riflemen from the frontier to serve in the new army. So many men volunteered that Washington had to find a way to choose between them. He took a board about 12 inches (30.48 cm) square and drew the shape of a nose in the center. He nailed the board to a tree 150 yards (137 m) away. Those who shot a bullet that hit closest to the mark were chosen. Almost all hit the mark.

Frontiersmen and farmers, their skills honed from shooting directly at a target during hunting, were excellent additions to the new army. With training and discipline, these skills became even greater assets.

For the Teacher

Project

Have a competition in marksmanship to choose a new militia.

Materials

- poster board
- marker
- thumb tack or masking tape
- small balls about 2 inches (5 cm) in diameter

Directions

1. Cut the poster board into a piece 12 inches (30.48 cm) square.
2. Use a marker to draw a nose in the center of the poster board.
4. Go outside and tack or tape the poster board target to a fence or solid object. Determine a safe distance away and give each "farmer" a chance to throw at the target and join the Revolutionary cause!

Seamen

Congress built a small navy of 50 to 60 ships and the colonies' navies added about another 40. These were commanded by local sea captains who recruited crews from their home ports. Americans at sea concentrated on defending American shores, harassing the enemy, and plundering British merchant ships. The British also dispatched a fleet of ships whose job was to patrol American coastlines and set up blockades.

Ships on both sides were packed with barrels containing lead balls for muskets. Other barrels were on board to hold water, wine, rum, and grain. Many seamen brought with them keepsakes, small objects that reminded them of home.

Project
Create a keepsake collage.

Materials
- magazines
- scissors
- construction paper
- glue

Directions
1. Imagine that you are boarding a ship that will take you out to sea to fight a war from which you might never return. What things would you want to have on board that would most remind you of home?
2. Draw or look through magazines for pictures of these things—special foods, pets, toys, etc.
3. Cut out the pictures and glue them in a collage on construction paper.

For the Teacher
Assemble the individual collages in one large mural on the classroom wall. Discuss the similarities and differences in the items selected.

Feeding the Army

George Washington estimated that he would need 100,000 barrels of flour and 20 million pounds (9,000 metric tons) of meat to feed 15,000 soldiers for one year. That quota was never met. The army often went hungry.

It was usually women and children who cooked for the soldiers. When battles were fought near their homes, they fed and cared for the wounded. Some women followed the army, acting as cooks and laundresses. One of the staples was biscuits, called *hardtack*, a mixture of only two ingredients—flour and water. It was tasteless, but had a long shelf life.

Project

Bake a batch of *hardtack*—biscuits served to Revolutionary armies.

Materials

- water
- flour
- small mixing bowl for each student
- waxed paper
- plastic glass or round cookie cutter
- plastic fork
- rolling pin

Directions

1. Add enough water to ¼ cup (60 ml) flour to make a soft, but not sticky, dough.

2. Punch and work the dough for about 10 minutes, until the dough is elastic in texture.

3. Roll out the dough on a sheet of waxed paper to ½-inch (1.27 cm) thickness.

4. Use a plastic glass or circle-shaped cookie cutter to cut the dough into biscuits. Prick each one with a fork.

5. Bake at 450° F (240° C) for about seven minutes. Turn the oven down to 350° F (175° C) and bake seven to 10 minutes more. The biscuits should be hard, like a rock. Try to enjoy! Imagine a diet of hardtack!

Canteen

At the onset of the war, some British and American officers carried the comforts of home with them into the military camp. But that changed quickly as the war progressed. Most Revolutionary troops lacked food, clothing, ammunition, and regulation supplies.

Since equipment and supplies were scarce, soldiers often brought household items, such as tinderboxes with flint and pouches for cartridges, into battle with them. Farmers brought the small wooden barrels they took to the fields when they mowed hay to use as canteens for water or a ration of rum! The owner's initials were usually carved into the side of his canteen.

Project
Make a keg-shaped "canteen."

Materials
- oatmeal box with lid
- wide masking tape
- brown tempera paint
- paintbrush
- cork
- scissors or dull knife
- permanent marker

Directions
1. Cut an opening the size of the cork in the center of the oatmeal box.
2. Cover the oatmeal box with masking tape. Paint the tape brown.
3. Insert the cork in the hole.
3. "Carve" your initials on your canteen with a marker.

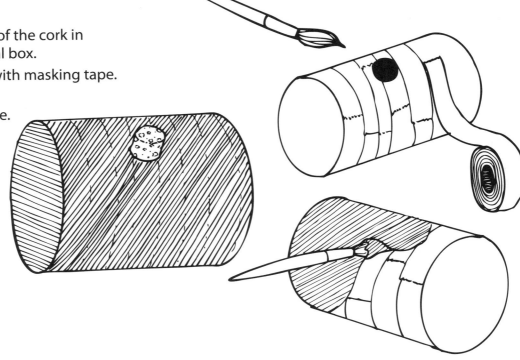

Redcoats

The British soldiers occupying American colonies were nicknamed *redcoats* because of their distinctive bright red uniforms. The uniforms of the colonists were almost identical in style, but were bright blue. In addition to uniform coats, soldiers wore light-colored breeches, boots, and tall hats.

However, many of the American fighters were dressed in makeshift uniforms, providing their own loose hunting shirts or homemade uniforms. Before the start of the war, George Washington, working as a surveyor in Indian lands, noticed that bright uniforms made soldiers very good targets—they were very easy to spot against the green of hillsides and forests. The everyday clothes of the militiamen made it much easier for them to defend their lands from behind trees and from other hidden positions.

Project

Make an illustration showing soldiers in different uniforms against a forest backdrop.

Materials

- book with illustrations of Revolutionary War uniforms, American and British
- drawing paper
- markers or crayons
- brown and green construction paper
- scissors
- thumb tacks

Directions

1. After researching uniforms, draw one of each soldier in uniform—redcoat, American regular (blue), and militia—on your paper.
2. Use markers or crayons to color your drawings.
3. Cut out your soldiers and post on the Revolutionary War landscape bulletin board.

For the Teacher

As a class, make a forest of trees out of construciton paper and pin to a bulletin board to create a Revolutionary War landscape bulletin board. After the students post their soldiers on the board, discuss with the class: Which uniform was the most practical? How were uniforms during the Revolutionary War similar or different to modern-day uniforms?

Elaborate Uniforms

The uniforms of both British and American officers could be very elaborate. Coats might be embellished with braid and *epaulettes*, or shoulder ornaments. Hats sometimes had feathers or *cockades*, which were decorative knots or rosettes made of ribbon.

A soldier's sword was a very important part of his uniform. The sword was carried in a leather shoulder strap called a *baldric*. Swords were sometimes decorated with a *sword knot*, a decorative tassel that was tied to the sword's hilt, or handle.

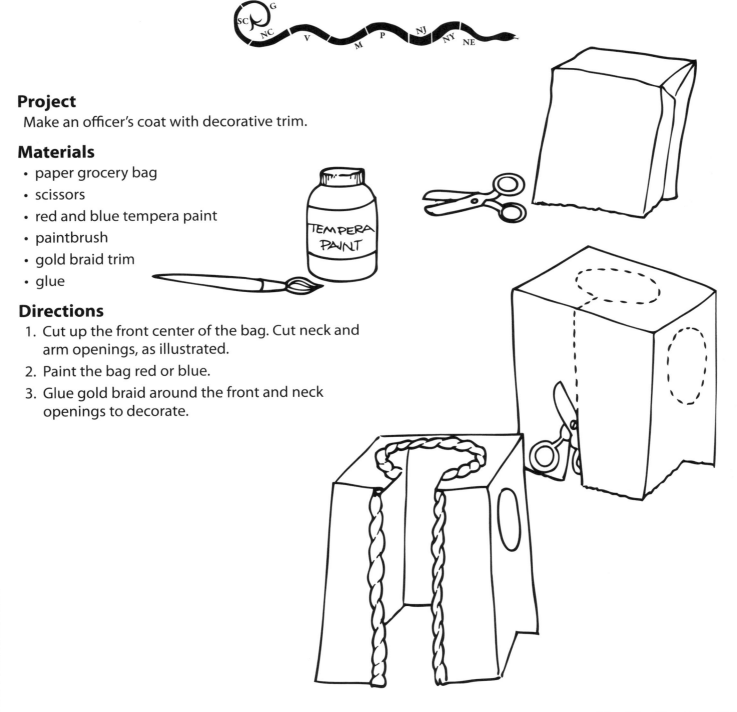

Project
Make an officer's coat with decorative trim.

Materials
- paper grocery bag
- scissors
- red and blue tempera paint
- paintbrush
- gold braid trim
- glue

Directions
1. Cut up the front center of the bag. Cut neck and arm openings, as illustrated.
2. Paint the bag red or blue.
3. Glue gold braid around the front and neck openings to decorate.

Fife and Drum

The British made up the song "Yankee Doodle" to insult the Americans. They said a "Yankee Doodle" was a person who was unsophisticated and didn't know how to fight. When the British marched to Lexington and Concord, they wore their red dress uniforms, and their drummers and pipers played "Yankee Doodle." After winning that battle, the Americans sang the song with pride. It became the most popular song of the American Revolution.

Fife (an instrument similar to a flute) and drums provided rousing music as well as signals on battlefields. Women expressed their support for the Revolution by singing patriotic songs at ceremonial functions.

Project

Make a fife and drums. Invite those who play flutes to join in with drummers and practice a military march to the tune "Yankee Doodle."

Materials

- large coffee can
- construction paper
- paper towel tube
- CD or tape player
- Recording of song "Yankee Doodle"
- glue
- yarn
- masking tape
- crayons
- scissors

Directions

Fife

1. Cut six holes in the top of a paper towel tube.
2. Wrap the tube ends with masking tape.

Drum

1. Measure construction paper the width of a coffee can. Cut a piece long enough to wrap around the can and cover it.
2. Color a patriotic symbol such as an eagle on the paper. Wrap the can and tape the paper in place.
3. Glue yarn, top to bottom, around the coffee can to create a zig-zag effect. Replace the lid.

For the Teacher

Have students who know how to play flutes or drums practice a military march to the tune "Yankee Doodle."

EP107 Revolutionary War Era © GHC Specialty Brands, LLC

Powder Horn

Along with his gun, a militiaman carried a cartridge pouch and a cow or ox horn in which he carried gunpowder. The powder horn was often the same one the soldier carried when hunting before the outbreak of war. On the powder horn he carved designs and pictures which usually included his name, the date and place it was carved, and a slogan reflecting the ideals of freedom.

Military records during the Revolution were sketchy, at best. It was often the powder horn, with its personal information, that provided the only way to identify a soldier who had died on the battlefield.

Project
Make a paper powder horn.

Materials
- white or tan construction paper
- thin-tipped black markers
- clear tape

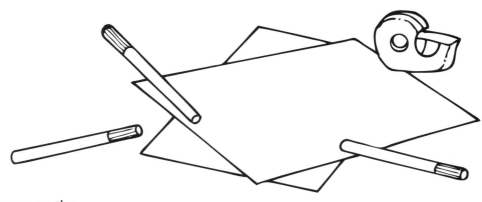

Directions
1. Use a black marker to create pictures on the |construction paper. Include date, name, and city.
2. Roll the paper to create a cone. Tape to hold in place.

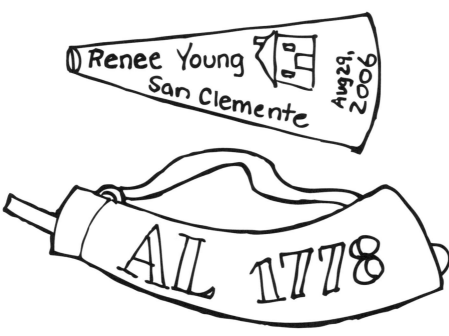

Valley Forge

The winter at Valley Forge has come to be symbolic of the hardships suffered by the American soldiers during the Revolutionary War. Washington and his men set up camp from December of 1777 through June of 1778 in this Pennsylvania location. To say conditions were miserable is to put it mildly.

Supplies were so scarce that blankets were the only thing many soldiers had to cover themselves. Men on guard duty borrowed clothing from their buddies who stayed behind by the fire in the huts. Many men did not have shoes—they left bloody footprints in the snow from marching on frozen ground. More than one soldier ended up having one or both legs amputated.

Food was also in short supply. This resulted in more than one-fourth of the soldiers dying of malnutrition, and of diseases such as smallpox, pneumonia, and influenza. Meanwhile, merchants in the surrounding areas were getting rich by holding commodities off the market to garner higher prices. Some even sold food to the British, leaving their own soldiers to starve.

Project

Imagine that you are one of the soldiers camped at Valley Forge. Create a diary and include written entries and drawings to illustrate the hardships the soldiers endured there. You might want to include a drawing of General Washington or a map of Valley Forge.

Materials

- research materials
- paper
- pen or pencil
- crayons or colored pencils
- colored construction paper

Directions

1. Fold construction paper in half and tuck several sheets of paper inside. Staple the spine of your diary.
2. Use research materials to find out more about the soldiers' stay at Valley Forge.
3. Fill your diary with entries, maps and sketches.
4. Share your diary by posting it on a bulletin board.

EP107 Revolutionary War Era © GHC Specialty Brands, LLC

Muskets and Rifles

Americans adapted the British musket known as "Brown Bess," decorated it with tiger stripes, and took it into battle. Muskets were heavy and inaccurate, so inaccurate that it was difficult to hit a target more than 100 yards (91.4 meters) away. But a musket could be fitted with a bayonet—a sharp sword attached to the end—and a rifle could not. Reloading a gun took time; the bayonet was deadly and could be used in close quarters. Soldiers stood in parallel lines and fired at each other. With each round they moved closer together until they were in hand-to-hand combat. Even though rifles were more accurate than muskets, their value was not recognized by officers on either side.

Project
Examine the difference between muskets and rifles by creating a Venn Diagram.

Materials
- white paper
- pencil or pen
- saucer
- reference materials

Directions
1. In an encyclopedia or other source, read how muskets and rifles were different.
2. Turn your saucer upside down on a sheet of white paper. Trace and draw two overlapping circles, as shown in the illustration.
3. Label the left circle "Muskets." Label the right circle "Rifles." In the middle, where the circles overlap, print "Both."
4. In the area below "Muskets," list features that pertained solely to this kind of weapon.
5. Do the same with "Rifles."
6. Under "Both" list features that pertained to both muskets and rifles.

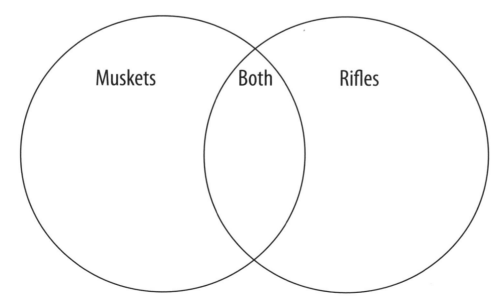

Boston Massacre

On March 5, 1770, an unruly mob of men and boys begain taunting a single British sentry on duty in front of the Customs House. Referring to the color of the British uniforms, the mob called out insults such as, "You lobsterbacks! Bloodybacks! Cowards!" Then the taunting escalated to the throwing of snowballs and rocks at the sentry. Eventually, the sentry was knocked to the ground and began calling for help.

British Captain Thomas Preston arrived with seven other soldiers, but he could not persuade the group of men and boys to disperse. Instead, the mob grew even larger. For over an hour the taunting continued, with the mob daring the soldiers to fire.

Crispus Attucks stood at the front of the mob, holding a stick of firewood and yelling insults as well. In fact, Attucks was so close at one point that a soldier's bayonet nearly touched him. He told his fellow Patriots not to fear, because the British would not fire. What happened next is not clear. A fight started, and perhaps because of all the commotion, shots rang out. Captain Preston maintained he did not order his men to shoot.

Crispus Attucks was the first to fall. When it was over, five people had been killed. The redcoats were arrested. A jury found that the soldiers acted in self-defense. Was it really a massacre?

Project
Write a newspaper article on the Boston Massacre.

Directions
1. Do some additional research. In small groups, discuss what you think really happened on March 5, 1770.

2. Then, write an article for a newspaper describing the Boston Massacre. Remember to include the "who, what, where, when, and how." Be sure you add a caption for the illustration and an eye-catching headline!

For the Teacher
Copy the illustration at right. Give one to each student to include in their article. Post all articles on a bulletin board.

Boston Tea Party

On the evening of December 16, 1773, a group of American colonists disguised as Native Americans boarded British ships in Boston Harbor and broke open 342 chests of tea, dumping the tea into the water. This event, which came to be known as the "Boston Tea Party," was a violent protest against British taxation in the colonies. It was the first aggressive act performed by the colonists on their quest for independence.

Tea was probably the most popular beverage in the colonies. When the British imposed heavy taxes on tea being imported to the colonies, the colonists rebelled by refusing to drink it. Tea was kept in wooden chests that were often ornate and beautifully decorated.

Project
Make a tea chest and sample different types of tea.

Materials
- large shoebox with lid
- brown tempera paint and paint brush
- scraps of brightly colored construction paper
- spray lacquer
- several varieties of tea bags
- foam cups

Directions
1. Paint shoebox and lid.
2. Cut designs from construction paper scraps and glue onto box.
3. Spray box with lacquer and let dry.
4. Place tea bags in box.

For the Teacher
Have a class tea-tasting party. Help students make different kinds of tea and serve in foam cups.

Paul Revere

Paul Revere was born in Boston, Massachusetts, on January 1, 1735. He was an expert silversmith, and was also well known for engraving and other types of metal work. After serving for a short time in the militia, he became a courier of information during the Revolutionary War.

Paul Revere is probably best known as one of the riders sent to warn the minutemen of the approach of British troops on the eve of the Battles of Lexington and Concord. On April 18, 1775, British redcoats set out by sea from Boston toward Concord. Patriot organizers hung two lanterns in the steeple of the Old North Church. Paul Revere saw the signal, and along with William Dawes, rode north to alert people in neighboring towns and villages.

Project
Make a paper lantern similar to the lanterns hung in the Old North Church.

Materials
- half-gallon (1.89 L) milk carton
- yellow construction paper
- black construction paper, cut in 1-inch (2.54-cm) strips
- glue
- scissors
- tape

Directions
1. Cut the top off of the milk carton to form a rectangular box.
2. Cut yellow construction paper to cover the outside of the box and tape into place.
3. Place black construction paper strips lengthwise at intervals around the box, being sure that strips of yellow show between the black strips. Glue into place. Trim any excess pieces.
4. Make a handle by gluing each end of a black strip to opposite edges of the top of the box.
5. Glue one black strip around the top edge of the box and a second strip around the bottom.

Paul Revere's Ride

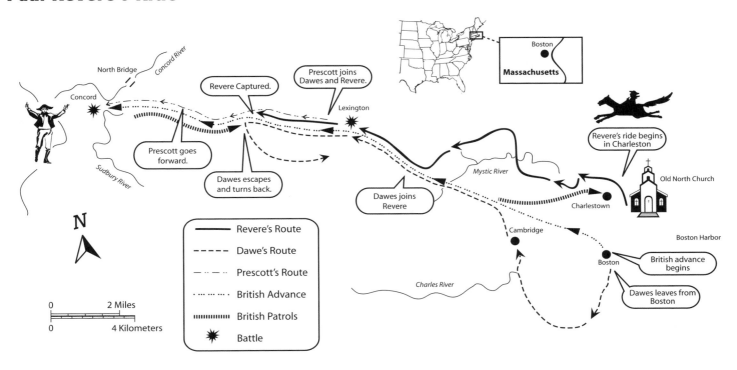

Project

Build geography skills by interpreting the map of Paul Revere's Ride.

Answer the following questions about the map.

1. Determine the distance between the Old North Church and: Lexington _____ . Concord _____ .

2. Where did battles take place? _____

3. How are the following routes symbolized on the map?

   Dawes's _____   Revere's _____

   British _____   Prescott's _____

4. Who was captured by the British? _____

5. Who managed to escape? _____

6. Who actually reached Concord with the message? _____

7. In what colony did the ride take place? _____

Declaration of Independence

The Declaration of Independence, written by Thomas Jefferson in about two weeks, is the document in which the American colonies declared their freedom from British rule. The Second Continental Congress, a meeting of delegates from all the colonies, adopted the Declaration on July 4, 1776. On July 19, Congress ordered the Declaration to be *engrossed* (written in beautiful script on parchment). The president of the Congress, John Hancock, was the first to sign. Eventually all 56 members of Congress signed.

The original parchment copy of the Declaration is housed in the National Archives Building in Washington, D.C. It is displayed with the United States Constitution and the Bill of Rights.

Project

Create a decorative mural that features each student's signature engrossed on a classroom "scroll."

Materials

- colored markers
- red or blue butcher paper
- white construction paper
- glue
- pencils

Directions

1. Sign your name on a sheet of white construction paper. Use pencil first so that erasures can be made and fancy flourishes can be added.

2. Decorate your signature with colored markers.

3. Glue your signature sheet to the butcher paper. Display on a classroom door or wall.

For the Teacher

On the chalkboard, create several examples of handwriting with flourishes on the letters.

Minutemen

In the years before the Revolutionary War, volunteers were organized into military companies and trained to bear arms. These men were called *minutemen* because they were prepared to fight "at a minute's notice."

On April 18, 1775, British Lieutenant General Thomas Gage ordered his redcoats to destroy the Patriots' main supply depot at Concord, Massachusetts. They arrived at Lexington early the next morning. A band of minutemen faced the redcoats on the village green. No one knows who fired the first shot, but eight colonists were killed and 10 wounded. Minutemen opposed the advancing British, spurring people from all walks of life to join the cause of liberty.

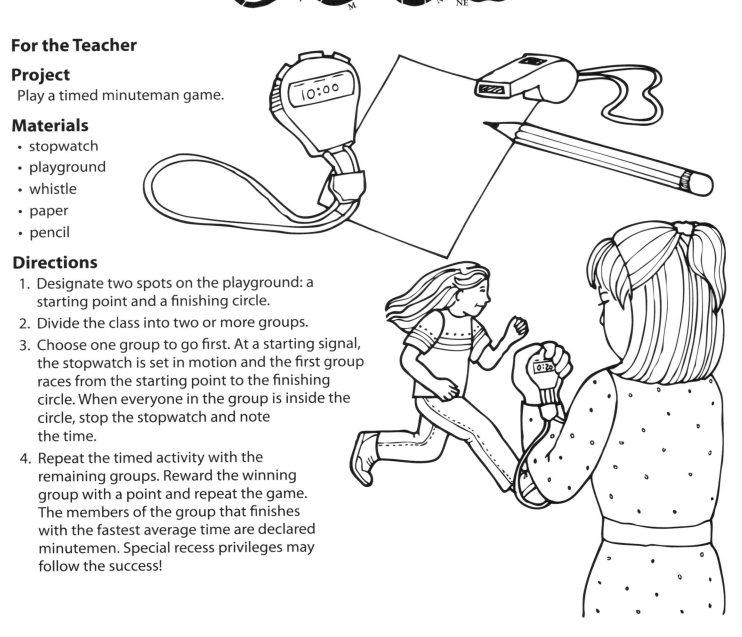

For the Teacher

Project
Play a timed minuteman game.

Materials
- stopwatch
- playground
- whistle
- paper
- pencil

Directions
1. Designate two spots on the playground: a starting point and a finishing circle.
2. Divide the class into two or more groups.
3. Choose one group to go first. At a starting signal, the stopwatch is set in motion and the first group races from the starting point to the finishing circle. When everyone in the group is inside the circle, stop the stopwatch and note the time.
4. Repeat the timed activity with the remaining groups. Reward the winning group with a point and repeat the game. The members of the group that finishes with the fastest average time are declared minutemen. Special recess privileges may follow the success!

George Washington

George Washington guided his country for more than 20 years during the Revolutionary era and became the chief symbol of what the colonists were fighting for. He commanded the Continental Army that won American independence. He served as president of the convention that wrote the United States Constitution. After the war it was suggested the Army set up a monarchy with Washington as king. He fought against the idea and eventually became the first man elected President of the United States.

Washington was loved by the people of his time. Especially after his death in 1799, his likeness was used on everything—cast iron stoves, statues, painting, and even chocolate candy molds.

For the Teacher

Project

Complete a project that features the likeness of George Washington.

Materials

- Washington Project Page (page 43)
- reference books featuring pictures of Washington
- colored pencils
- watercolor paints
- crayons
- tempera paints
- glue
- cardboard boxes
- scissors
- poster board
- small gift boxes
- paintbrushes

Directions

1. Set up three areas in the classroom for the completion of each project. Provide the necessary materials at each area. Stock a central table with reference books featuring George Washington.

2. Copy one Washington Project Page (43) per student.

3. Allow students to go to the project area of their choice.

Washington Project Page

Miniature

Miniatures, or small portraits, appeared on candy boxes, snuff boxes, and pins. George Washington's profile was a popular image for many miniatures.

Materials
- poster board
- colored pencils
- small gift box
- scissors
- glue

Directions
1. Cut a small oval from poster board.
2. Sketch and color a profile of Washington's head on the oval to create a miniature.
3. Glue the miniature to the lid of the gift box.

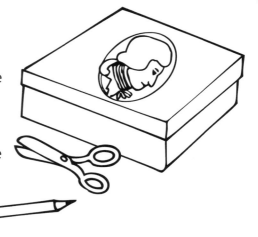

Statue

Washington has been honored in monuments and statues. The only statue for which he posed is carved from marble, by Jean Houdon.

Materials
- poster board
- cardboard
- tempera paint
- scissors
- glue

Directions
1. Cut a body shape from cardboard. Paint the figure of George Washington on the cardboard.
2. Cut a poster board triangle. Fold it in half, and glue one half to the back of the figure so it will stand.

Painting

Historical events during the Revolutionary era were recreated in paintings. Many featured George Washington in memorable moments from his life and military career.

Materials
- white construction paper
- watercolor paints

Directions
1. Look through reference books for paintings featuring George Washington.
2. Use the paintings, plus information you know about the Revolutionary War, to paint a picture that features George Washington.

Native Americans

There were Native American supporters for both the Patriots and the British during the Revolutionary War. Many tribes allied themselves with the redcoats in hopes of stopping the spread of the frontiersmen into their lands. These alliances were often sealed with the giving of valuable gifts such as silver ornaments.

On the other hand, Oneidas of western New York aided the Americans during the terrible winter at Valley Forge, sending snowshoes to the American soldiers. Both the British and the Americans paid Native Americans for scalps taken from the enemy. A few Native Americans actually became soldiers in one of the opposing armies.

Project

Make an ornamental armlet similar to ornaments given to the Native Americans by the British.

Materials

- poster board, cut in 3-inch (7.6-cm) strips
- aluminum foil
- toothpick
- tape

Directions

1. Cut a poster board strip to fit loosely around upper arm, plus a 1-inch (2.54 cm) overlap.
2. Adjust fit and tape ends of strip together. Cut a scalloped or decorative edge.
3. Cover band with aluminum foil.
4. Use toothpick to trace decorative patterns on the aluminum foil to resemble engraving.

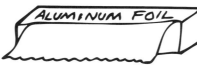

A National Flag

At the start of the Revolutionary War, Americans fought under many different flags. After the Declaration of Independence, the British flag was no longer appropriate. In 1777, the Continental Congress issued a resolve defining the elements to be incorporated into a national flag: red, white, and blue; stars and stripes. No specific design came about until several decades later.

No one knows who made the first flag. Congressman Francis Hopkinson claimed that he had designed it. Legend has it that Betsy Ross, a Philadelphia seamstress, made the first U.S. flag. Most historians do not support this claim.

Project
Design the "first" national flag.

Materials
- red, white, and blue construction paper
- large sheet white construction paper
- scissors
- glue

Directions
1. Imagine it is your job to design the first national flag of the United States.
2. Keeping the designated elements in mind (red, white, and blue; stars and stripes), cut and glue construction paper to create a unique flag.

For the Teacher
Display all the designs. In a "session of Congress," have students vote on an official national flag from the ones displayed.

Loyalists

Loyalists were colonists who remained loyal to Great Britain during the Revolution. Loyalists were made up of all different kinds of people, and they all had their own reasons for staying dedicated to the crown. Some of the most common reasons were political principles, emotional bonds to England, and fear of change. Most Loyalists distrusted democracy, which they believed would lead to unprotected citizens and political disorder. Reverend Mather Byles once questioned, "Which is better—to be ruled by one tyrant three thousand miles away or by three thousand tyrants one mile away?"

Patriots viewed the Loyalists as traitors who turned against their neighbors and fellow citizens to support a foreign rule. The Patriots designed laws to punish Loyalists and many were cast out from their communities. Loyalists viewed Patriots as radicals who were betraying their country and setting themselves up for their own failure.

For the Teacher

Project
Hold a Patriots vs. Loyalists debate.

Materials
- research materials

Directions
1. Divide the class into two groups—the Patriot and Loyalist parties.

2. Have each group research their position. After researching, discuss within the group how the party felt and why they felt that way.

3. Line up desks to face each other, Patriots on one side, Loyalists on the other. Have a debate. Get things started by asking, "Should the colonies separate from Great Britain and why?"

4. More talking points include—"Can democracy work in America?" "Should Great Britain allow America to rule themselves?" etc.

5. After the debate, have a follow-up discussion with the class. Did both sides do a good job of defending their opinions? Which side had the strongest arguments?

Literature List

Betrayal at Cross Creek
by Kathleen Ernst. Pleasant Co. Publications, 2004.160 p. Gr. 4–7
Twelve-year-old Elspeth Monro, a Scottish settler and weaver's apprentice on the North Carolina frontier in 1775, must find out who is betraying her Loyalist family during the months before the start of the Revolutionary War.

George Washington, Spymaster: How the Americans Outspied the British and Won the Revolutionary War
by Thomas B. Allen. National Geographic Children's Books, 2004. 196 p. Gr. 6–8
This biography of Revolutionary War General and first President of the United States, George Washington, focuses on his use of spies to gather intelligence that helped the colonies win the war.

Give Me Liberty: The Story of the Declaration of Independence
by Russell Freedman. Holiday House, 2002. 90 p. Gr. 4–8
Describes the events leading up to the Declaration of Independence as well as the personalities and politics behind its framing. Readers may also enjoy *Freedman's In Defense of Liberty: The Story of America's Bill of Rights* (Holiday House, 2003).

Hero of the High Seas: John Paul Jones and the American Revolution
by Michael Cooper. National Geographic Children's Books, 2006. 128 p. Gr. 4–7
The biography of Jones, who arrived in America on the eve of the War for Independence, and went on to serve in the Continental Navy. The arc of his exciting life's narrative led him to deliver the sting of war to the British people.

Johnny Tremain
by Esther Forbes. Yearling, reissue, 1980. 336 p. Gr. 5–9
After injuring his hand, a silversmith's apprentice in Boston becomes a messenger for the Sons of Liberty in the days before the American Revolution. Newbery Medal.

Let It Begin Here: Lexington and Concord, First Battles of the Revolutionary War
by Dennis Brindell Fradin. Walker & Co., 2005. 32 p. Gr. 2–4
The story of how the American Revolution started in April 1775 is told with drama and immediacy, accompanied by vivid illustrations.

Liberty or Death: The American Revolution, 1763–1783.
by Betsy and Giulio Maestro. HarperCollins, 2005. 64 p. Gr. 3–5
Simple narrative and colorful illustrations tell the story of the American Revolution.

Paul Revere's Midnight Ride
by Steven Krensky. HarperCollins, 2002. 32 p. Gr. 2–5
Lovely picture book retelling of Revere's ride to warn the colonists of the British troops.

The Signers: The 56 Stories Behind the Declaration of Independence
by Dennis Brindell Fradin. Walker & Co. 156 p. Gr. 4–6
Profiles each of the 56 men who signed the Declaration of Independence, giving historical information about the colonies they represented. Includes the text of the Declaration and its history.

They Called Her Molly Pitcher
by Anne Rockwell. Knopf Books for Young Readers, 2002. 40 p. Gr. 2–5
The story of the spirited Molly Pitcher who followed her husband when he joined General Washington's army.

You Wouldn't Want to Be at the Boston Tea Party: Wharf Water You'd Rather Not Drink
by Peter Cook. Franklin Watts, 2006. 32 p. Gr. 3–6
Amusing account that explores aspects of life during the Boston Tea Party—complete with handy hints and step-by-step guides.

Glossary

apprentice—one who agrees to work in a trade in exchange for instruction in that trade

baldric—leather shoulder strap worn across the chest to hold a sword or bugle

Boston Tea Party—a protest against British taxation in which colonists raided a British ship and dumped its load of tea into the harbor

canteen—a container used to hold water

churn—wooden or earthenware keg used for making butter

cockades—decorative knots or rosettes made of ribbon on uniform hats

colonist—a person who settles or lives in a colony

Crispus Attucks—the first person to fall at the Boston Massacre

epaulette—shoulder decoration, such as gold braid, on a military uniform

engrossed—written in large ornate script, often on parchment

fife—a flute-like instrument

flatboats—large, flat-bottomed barges or rafts used to carry passengers and belongings downriver

freeholders—settlers in American who were granted land

handbill—a single page of news posted on trees or tavern doors

hardtack—a type of biscuit consisting of only two ingredients, flour and water

journeyman—one who is qualified to work in a trade or craft

Lexington—the scene of the first battle of the American Revolution

linsey-woolsey—fabric that was a combination of linen and wool

master—a craftsman skilled in his trade who owns his own business

militia—a supplemental army made up of civilians

minutemen—colonists prepared to fight at a minute's notice

Paul Revere—a silversmith known for his ride to warn the minutemen of the approach of British troops

porringer—small shallow bowl, usually crafted from pewter

redcoats—British soldiers, so called because of the color of their uniforms

sampler—small strip of fabric embroidered with various designs

spider—long-handled, iron skillet that stood on three legs

Tree of Liberty—symbol of a giant elm tree representing the American Revolution

tricorn hats—three-cornered hats.

Valley Forge—campsite in Pennsylvania where Washington's army spent the winter of 1777 in extremely harsh conditions

yeoman—farmer who cultivates his own land